MAHLIA AMATINA

Dear Manager

First edition

ISBN: 978-1-9195538-6-3

Editing by Grace Gilbert
Cover art by Erin Caitlin Karn (using licensed Canva elements)

This book was professionally typeset on Reedsy.
Find out more at reedsy.com

Contents

1

Introduction: Why Supporting Autistic Employees Matters

Dear Manager,

Let me begin with a truth that sits right at the heart of this book: supporting autistic employees isn't just good for us, it's good for *everyone.*

I've spent years navigating workplaces that weren't designed for minds like mine. I've worked in all types of settings and industries, and, despite the differences in job roles or businesses, one thing has remained painfully consistent: a deep misunderstanding of what autism actually looks like in the workplace.

The Quiet Cost of Not Understanding Autism

It's hard to overstate the impact this misunderstanding has. According to the Office for National Statistics (2021), just 29% of autistic adults are in employment, the lowest employment rate among any disabled group. Even among those who do work, many are underemployed, mismanaged or stuck in roles that fail to utilise their strengths.

But What Do These Statistics Mean in Practice?

It means an autistic graduate who's spent years honing their craft is never given a chance because they "didn't smile enough" in an interview.

It means an autistic employee who's brilliant with data but struggles with office small talk is viewed as "antisocial" or "difficult."

It means years of masking, burnout and resignation, not because we're incapable, but because systems haven't adapted to us.

And it's not that autistic people lack motivation or talent. Far from it. Many of us are creative thinkers, hyper-focused problem solvers, incredibly loyal team members and are passionate about our work. But without the right understanding and support, our contributions are often missed or misunderstood.

What I Wish My Past Managers Had Known

Looking at my own career journey to date, there are so many moments I wish my managers had seen me more clearly, not just as someone "struggling" but as someone differently wired, with a unique perspective that could have benefited the whole team.

I once had a role where I consistently overdelivered on projects, yet I was told I was "too quiet in meetings". No one ever asked why I was quiet or if meetings were accessible to me. No one asked if I processed information differently, or if I'd prefer to give input in writing. Instead, my silence was interpreted as disengagement.

The truth? I was overstimulated, processing multiple voices and conflicting signals, and struggling to find a gap in the rapid-fire conversation to share my thoughts.

I internalised those moments. I tried to force myself into being more "dynamic", more "present", more "normal". And it led me to burnout, not once, but several times throughout my career.

What Would Have Helped?

1. A manager who took the time to check in with me directly and ask how I preferred to communicate
2. A team culture that valued different types of contributions
3. The permission to be myself, without fear of being labelled "unprofessional" for needing rest, routine or quiet

Beyond Legal Obligations: The Human Case for Inclusion

In Great Britain, the Equality Act 2010 legally requires employers to make reasonable adjustments for disabled people experiencing long-term effects on daily life, including autistic employees. But I want us to aim higher than legal minimums.

When workplaces embrace neurodivergence, when they value different ways of thinking, sensing and working, they become more inclusive, more creative and more effective. In fact, companies that prioritise diversity (including neurodiversity) are 35% more likely to outperform competitors (McKinsey, 2020).

And this isn't just about performance metrics, it's about humanity.

It's about recognising that autistic employees aren't problems to be solved, but people to be understood.

It's about moving away from a deficit-based view of autism, and toward a strengths-based, individualised, relational understanding.

It's about making space for everyone, not just those who fit the corporate mould.

What You'll Find in This Book

This book isn't a clinical guide. It's not filled with jargon or abstract theories. It's a practical, compassionate toolkit designed to support you in becoming a more inclusive and effective manager.

You'll also find:

- First-hand insights from me as an autistic employee and advocate
- Real-life case studies and scenarios to bring the learning to life
- Research-backed strategies for inclusive leadership
- Reflection questions to deepen your understanding and practice
- Clear definitions of terms like intersectionality, masking, burnout and more

Everything is written accessibly, so that whether you're new to autism or already on your inclusion journey, you'll feel supported and empowered to take action.

This Work Is Urgent and It's Ongoing

We are at a pivotal moment in workplace culture. Neurodiversity is gaining recognition, but often in superficial ways. Awareness without action leads nowhere. To truly support your autistic employees, you need more than just training videos and policy templates. You need to unlearn, listen deeply and lead with humility.

That might sound daunting, but I promise you, it's worth it.

Because when autistic people are supported, *really* supported, we don't just survive. We thrive. We innovate. We stay. We grow.

And we bring our full selves to work, enriching the team in ways you may never have imagined.

So, Manager: thank you for reading this far.

Thank you for being open.
Thank you for being ready to lead differently.
Let's build something better, together.

Reflection Questions

1. What assumptions or stereotypes do I currently hold, consciously or unconsciously, about autism in the workplace?
2. Can I recall a time when I misunderstood or misjudged a colleague who might have been neurodivergent?
3. How willing am I to challenge traditional workplace norms in order to create a more inclusive environment?
4. What does inclusion look like in practice, not just in policy, in my team or department?
5. Am I ready to move from "awareness" to real, actionable change?

2

Understanding Autism in the Workplace

Getting Beyond the Stereotypes to See Autistic People as We Are

Dear Manager,

When you hear the word autism, what comes to mind?

For many managers I've spoken with, it's a child with specialist support needs. Or maybe the lone tech genius with awkward social skills, someone like Sheldon Cooper or a "Rain Man" type figure. Though slowly changing, these are the kinds of stereotypes that dominate the media, and they shape how autism is perceived across society, including in the workplace.

But autism isn't one thing. And it certainly doesn't end at childhood.

We grow up. We go to university. We apply for jobs. We walk into your offices. We sit in your teams. And often, we do all of this while hiding significant aspects of who we are, just to survive a system not built for us.

What Is Autism, Really?

Autism is a neurodevelopmental difference that affects how a person experiences the world. It influences how we process sensory input, communicate, relate socially and manage changes in routine. Some people may also have differences in movement, executive functioning (planning and organisation) or how emotions are experienced and expressed.

Neurodevelopmental means it's something we're born with; our brains are simply wired differently. This isn't a disorder to be "fixed". It's a natural part of human diversity. And many autistic people, including myself, proudly identify as neurodivergent: a term that describes those whose brain works differently from the so-called "neurotypical" majority.

This isn't about being better or worse: just different.

Autism exists across a spectrum, not a linear one from mild to severe, but a multidimensional spectrum. Each person has a unique profile of strengths, needs, challenges and preferences. Some of us may communicate verbally, others non-speaking. Some may have strong visual thinking skills, others may excel with patterns, logic or empathy.

You likely can't tell if someone is autistic. In fact, many of us go undiagnosed for years, especially women, people of colour and those who don't fit the outdated stereotypes. I wasn't diagnosed until adulthood, despite always feeling "different" in school, at university, and eventually, in the workplace.

The problem wasn't me. The problem was that autism has long been defined in relation to white, male, cisgender and often middle-class experiences.

Why Is This Relevant at Work?

Because the workplace wasn't designed with neurodivergent people in mind.

So many of us enter jobs full of passion, skill and ideas, only to be met with confusion, miscommunication, and misunderstanding. We're seen as "too intense", "too quiet", "too blunt", or "not a team player." But these labels miss the context.

We're often processing sensory overload.

Or translating unclear expectations.

Or masking our natural responses so we can appear more acceptable.

Quick Definitions:

1. **Masking**: The act of consciously or unconsciously suppressing autistic behaviours (like stimming, avoiding eye contact or using direct language) to fit into neurotypical norms. Masking is exhausting and is linked to anxiety, depression and burnout.
2. **Stimming**: Self-stimulatory behaviours like rocking, hand-flapping or fidgeting, which help us regulate emotions or sensory input. These are often misunderstood but are actually healthy coping tools.
3. **Neurodivergent**: A term encompassing a variety of neurological differences, such as autism, ADHD, dyslexia, dyspraxia and more.
4. **Neurotypical**: People whose brain development and functioning align with societal norms: essentially, the majority group.

The Workplace Stats

The numbers are stark:

- Only 29% of autistic adults in the UK are in any kind of employment (ONS, 2021).
- Over 50% of autistic employees report not feeling comfortable disclosing their diagnosis to their employer (National Autistic Society, 2021).
- 71% of autistic people say they've experienced workplace discrimination or barriers (National Autistic Society, 2021).

And yet, there's also huge potential:

- In one study, neurodivergent teams were 30% more productive when properly supported (CIPD, 2021).
- Autistic professionals often bring hyper-focus, deep integrity, creative problem-solving and systemic thinking - all vital assets in today's workforce.

So why is there such a gap between our potential and our actual experiences?

Because the systems haven't caught up. We're expected to adapt to workplaces, instead of workplaces adapting to us.

My Lived Experience: "You're Too Direct"

I once had a job where I was repeatedly told that my communication style was "too direct". I was just being clear and concise, which is often how autistic people prefer to communicate. But because I wasn't sugar-coating my messages or using lots of small talk, I was seen as abrupt.

Instead of being valued for my clarity, I was criticised for my tone.

This meant I started second-guessing every email, every meeting comment, every conversation. I'd spend hours editing what I wrote to make it sound "friendlier", even when that didn't feel authentic. That's a form of masking too, and it's exhausting.

What could have helped?

- A conversation about communication preferences
- An understanding that autistic people often value honesty and efficiency
- A shift in the team culture to embrace different communication styles rather than penalise them

Case Study: Navigating an Open Plan Office

I once supported an autistic employee, let's call her Zara, who was thriving in her role as a data analyst. She had an incredible eye for detail and consistently produced high-quality work. But she was placed in a large, buzzing open-plan office: a setting that became one of her biggest barriers. Constant interruptions from colleagues, background chatter, the hum of printers and the harsh glare of fluorescent lights all combined into daily sensory overwhelm.

At first, her manager misread the situation. Instead of considering Zara's environment, he assumed her performance dip meant she was disengaged or struggling with workload. This was a missed opportunity: by jumping to conclusions about her motivation rather than exploring underlying causes, he inadvertently added pressure and made Zara feel undervalued. As a result, her stress levels grew, and she began taking more sick days.

The turning point came when her manager, after noticing the pattern and being prompted by HR, finally arranged a one-to-one meeting. This time, he approached with openness and compassion, creating a safe space where Zara felt able to explain what was really happening. For the first time, she shared how overwhelming the office environment was, and how much it impacted her ability to focus.

Once the real issue was on the table, small adjustments made a huge difference. The manager agreed to noise-cancelling headphones, adjusted the overhead lighting near her desk and allowed her to work from home twice a week. These changes didn't cost much, but they had a transformational impact. Zara's productivity and confidence bounced back, her sick days reduced, and she even went on to become a mentor for other neurodivergent colleagues - sharing strategies and showing that autistic employees can flourish when workplaces adapt.

What stands out here is the contrast between poor and good practice. Initially, assumptions and a lack of awareness led to stress and burnout risk. But when her manager finally took the time to listen, believe and act, the outcome was positive for everyone: Zara, her manager, and the wider team.

Zara didn't need fixing. The environment did.

Autism Is Not a Deficit

I want to be very clear about something: autism is not a lack. It's a difference. And when you view it that way, you begin to see autistic employees not as "difficult", but as dynamic thinkers who may just need a different path to arrive.

Yes, there may be challenges. But those challenges are almost always environmental, relational or rooted in misunderstanding, not internal flaws.

Avoiding One-Size-Fits-All Thinking

It's tempting to look for a checklist: "What do autistic employees need?" But the answer isn't a formula, it's individual conversations and flexibility.

Some of us want lots of structure. Others want creative freedom.

Some thrive with routine. Others enjoy variety.

Some want quiet workspaces. Others prefer music or background noise.

The common thread? We want to be listened to and taken seriously.

To support autistic employees well, you don't need to be a clinician or an expert in neurodiversity. What you do need is:

- Curiosity
- A willingness to challenge your assumptions
- Commitment to inclusive practices
- A belief that diversity includes brain diversity too

And if you're unsure? Just ask us. We're the experts on our own experiences.

Reflection Questions

1. What image comes to mind when I think of autism? Where might that image come from?
2. Have I ever judged a colleague's behaviour (e.g., being blunt, avoiding eye contact, not engaging in small talk) without considering a neurodivergent perspective?
3. How might I shift my understanding of autism from a deficit-based model to a difference-based one?
4. What small steps can I take to better recognise and support neuro-

divergent people in my team?

5. Am I making space for autistic people to define their own needs, or am I assuming I already know?

3

Creating an Inclusive Culture

Why Culture Matters More Than Checklists

Dear Manager,

Let me be honest with you. Most of the autistic people I know don't leave jobs because of the workload, or even because of the formal policies.

We leave because of culture.

It's not usually the job that breaks us, it's the *unwritten rules*, the subtle exclusions, the team dynamics we're never quite invited into.

We notice when colleagues stop CC'ing us on emails.

We feel it when everyone else is chatting after the meeting, but no one looks our way.

We sense when our contributions are treated like interruptions rather than insights.

It's not always malicious. But it adds up.

You might be surprised how often autistic employees are left out socially or professionally, not because they aren't capable or contributing, but because they don't intuitively conform to team norms that were never made with them in mind.

So, let's explore what it really means to create an inclusive workplace culture: one where we feel seen, safe and supported.

What Do We Mean by "Inclusive Culture"?

When we talk about workplace culture, we're not just talking about whether you have a table tennis table or diversity policies in a binder.

Workplace culture is:

- How people interact when no one's watching
- What behaviours get rewarded and what gets ignored
- Who feels they belong and who doesn't

An inclusive culture is one where difference is not just accepted; it's welcomed, respected and woven into the way things are done. Where people don't have to conform to thrive. Where everyone is treated equitably, not identically.

Let's be clear about the difference:

- Equality means treating everyone the same
- Equity means giving people what they need to succeed, even if that looks different from what others receive

This is vital for autistic employees. Because treating us "just like everyone else" often means ignoring our actual needs.

Why Culture Matters More Than Policy

You could have all the right policies in place: reasonable adjustments, a Diversity, Equity and Inclusion (DEI) strategy, even a neurodiversity hiring initiative. But if your culture doesn't match, autistic employees won't stick around.

In fact, according to research by CIPD (2021), over 70% of neurodivergent employees say the workplace culture is a bigger barrier than the tasks of the job itself.

What does this look like in real life?

- An autistic colleague is told the office is "inclusive" but is then mocked for bringing their own lunch to avoid sensory overwhelm in canteens.
- A manager shares their support for neurodiversity publicly but consistently excludes the autistic team member from brainstorming meetings because they "don't contribute to the right energy".
- A team has an "open-door" policy, but autistic employees are penalised for preferring communication in writing rather than spontaneous drop-ins.

In each of these examples, the barrier isn't a lack of policy: it's a lack of psychological safety.

What Is Psychological Safety?

Psychological safety is the belief that you won't be humiliated or punished for showing up as yourself. It's when you feel safe to say:

- "I don't know"
- "I need help"
- "That process doesn't work for me"
- "I'm autistic, and here's what supports me best"

For autistic employees, psychological safety means we don't have to constantly mask our needs, suppress our stims or pretend we're coping when we're not. It means we trust our manager will respond with curiosity instead of criticism.

My Experience: Culture Without Inclusion

I once worked for a company that proudly displayed their "diversity credentials" on the website. They talked about celebrating difference, and there were even internal webinars about neurodiversity.

But in practice, when I struggled with the open office layout and asked to work in a quieter space, I was told I needed to be "more flexible". When I suggested a more structured meeting agenda to help me prepare, I was dismissed as being "too rigid".

That kind of mismatch, between stated values and actual culture, is incredibly disheartening. It sends a message that difference is only welcome when it's convenient.

And that's not inclusion. That's conditional tolerance.

The Power of Proactive Inclusion

True inclusion doesn't wait for someone to burn out. It doesn't require people to disclose a diagnosis in order to be treated with respect.

Proactive inclusion means creating systems and cultures where people don't have to fight for their basic needs.

This might include:

- Structured meeting agendas sent in advance for everyone
- Multiple ways to participate (e.g., via chat, written notes, 1:1 follow-ups)
- Quiet spaces where people can decompress
- Celebrating different communication styles, not punishing them
- Training your whole team to understand neurodiversity, not just HR

Case Study: Team Culture Shift

I worked with an organisation where one autistic employee, Jamal, struggled to engage in brainstorming sessions. He was deeply thoughtful, but slow to speak up in high-energy, fast-paced discussions. The team assumed he didn't have any ideas.

After we introduced asynchronous brainstorming, giving team members the chance to contribute ideas in a shared document before the meeting, Jamal's input tripled. Not only did he share more ideas, but his ideas were some of the most innovative and well-researched.

Soon, others on the team started preferring that method too.

It turns out neuroinclusive design isn't just for autistic employees: it helps everyone.

That's the power of inclusive culture. It creates conditions for everyone to succeed, not just the loudest or most extroverted voices.

Inclusion Happens in the Small Moments

A kind word after a team meeting.

A manager who checks in after a change in routine.

A colleague who doesn't make a joke at our expense.

A celebration that doesn't always revolve around alcohol or forced socialising.

These may seem small to you.

To us, they mean everything.

Watch for Cultural Red Flags

If you're not sure whether your team culture is truly inclusive, look for these warning signs:

- High turnover among neurodivergent or "quiet" team members
- "We've always done it this way" thinking
- Social events that exclude people with sensory, dietary or social differences
- Unconscious bias in who gets praised, promoted or heard
- A lack of neurodivergent voices in decision-making

Remember: if autistic people are present but not thriving, something needs to change.

Inclusion Is Everyone's Responsibility

Creating an inclusive culture isn't just the job of HR or leadership. It's *everyone's* responsibility.

But you, as a manager, set the tone. When you model inclusion, your team will follow. When you normalise asking about needs, others will too. When you show vulnerability, you give others permission to be human.

And that's really what this is about: recognising the full humanity of your autistic colleagues, without asking them to hide, shrink or change who they are.

It doesn't have to be perfect. You just have to start.

Ask questions. Listen deeply. Be willing to change. That's how inclusion begins.

Not with a banner or a buzzword, but with humility, courage and care.

Reflection Questions

1. In my team, who feels like they fully belong, and who might not?
2. What subtle messages might I be sending (intentionally or not) about what's valued?

3. Am I creating a psychologically safe space where all team members, especially autistic ones, can speak up, ask for help or be themselves?
4. How do I currently respond to differences in communication, pace or participation styles?
5. What's one small, practical change I could make to build a more inclusive team culture starting this week?

4

Effective Communication with Autistic Employees

Building Understanding Through Clear, Respectful and Supportive Dialogue

Dear Manager,

Let's talk about something that might sound simple but can feel like a daily minefield for many autistic employees: communication.

It's not that we can't communicate; we absolutely can, but we often communicate differently. And when those differences aren't recognised, respected or accommodated, it can create unnecessary misunderstandings, stress and even performance concerns.

In this chapter, I want to gently unpack some of the most common communication differences, share real examples from my own experience and offer you practical tools to make your communication more inclusive and effective.

Understanding Autistic Communication Differences

Autistic people tend to communicate in ways that are clear, direct and honest. Many of us avoid small talk, speak with literal interpretations or might take longer to process verbal information; not because we're being difficult, but because our brains are wired for depth and precision rather than nuance or subtext.

This can sometimes clash with neurotypical expectations, where communication is often layered with tone, implied meanings or social niceties that don't directly convey the message. That's where problems can start.

For example:

- If a manager says, "We might want to look at this again later", an autistic employee might interpret that as optional or non-urgent; when the manager really meant, "I need you to revise this by tomorrow."
- If feedback is given vaguely, e.g., "Can you be a bit more proactive?", we may not understand what precisely needs to change.

This isn't about lacking intelligence. It's about needing clarity. And clarity, when offered, can unlock some of our greatest strengths.

In fact, a 2023 study by the LSE's Centre for Economic Performance found that autistic employees thrive in workplaces that prioritise clear expectations and structured feedback. It's not autism that's the barrier; it's unclear communication.

My Experience: "Why Didn't You Just Ask?"

In one role, I was struggling with a particular software tool that the team used for project planning. I didn't find it intuitive, and every time I tried to use it, I ended up feeling overwhelmed and anxious.

But I didn't say anything. I didn't know how to bring it up without sounding like I was being difficult or incapable.

After several weeks, my manager asked me why I wasn't engaging with the platform. I hesitantly explained that I was having trouble navigating it and didn't find it accessible. He looked surprised and said, "Oh! You should have just said something, we could have trained you differently or let you use a different tool."

But the truth is, I couldn't "just say something". Not without the right culture. Not without being invited in.

We need psychologically safe environments where autistic employees feel like our needs won't be dismissed or used against us. That starts with managers who ask clear, open-ended questions and create communication routines that are inclusive by design.

Email Is a Lifeline

While some of us are comfortable with verbal communication, many of us (me included) prefer written communication like email or messaging platforms.

Why?

- It gives us time to process
- We can review the information more than once
- It reduces the pressure of immediate responses
- We're more likely to understand what's being asked

Please don't assume a delayed response means we're being evasive. We're often just taking time to formulate our thoughts clearly, because we very much want to get it right.

Providing options for communication, e.g. following up meetings with a written summary, or offering a choice between email or phone call, can make an enormous difference to autistic employees.

Meetings: Overwhelming, Not Unwilling

Many autistic people find meetings difficult. It's not because we don't care, it's because:

- There's often sensory overload (voices, visuals, room dynamics)
- Verbal turn-taking is hard to navigate
- We may not know when or how to jump in
- We're processing what's been said and may miss the moment to respond

I've sat through so many meetings feeling like my thoughts were trapped behind a pane of glass; I had ideas, questions, contributions, but couldn't find the right moment to speak.

The meeting would end, and I'd feel frustrated and invisible.

A more inclusive approach might be:

- Sending an agenda in advance
- Offering time at the end for anyone who hasn't spoken
- Allowing post-meeting contributions via email or chat
- Encouraging turn-taking and structured participation

These aren't big changes, but they send a powerful message: your input matters, and we're willing to meet you where you are.

Avoiding Assumptions and Reading Between the Lines

Many autistic employees don't mask their feelings through tone or facial expression in the same way neurotypical people do. You might not see frustration, excitement or confusion in the ways you expect.

Please don't read into this. Ask. Clarify. Don't assume that silence means agreement or that eye contact means engagement.

Equally, don't expect us to "read between the lines". If something is important, just say it clearly. If feedback is needed, give it with specificity.

I once had a manager say, "I expected you to know that was a priority." But no one had told me. And because I couldn't read the subtle office cues or unspoken urgency, I missed it and was unfairly penalised.

A Case Study: Talia's Feedback Loop

Talia, a 31-year-old autistic employee working in digital marketing, found her regular 1:1 meetings with her manager increasingly stressful. Instead of constructive input, she was often given vague reassurance such as, *"You're doing fine, just keep going!"* On the surface, this might have seemed supportive, but in practice it was poor management. The lack of specific feedback left Talia guessing what was expected of her, uncertain about whether she was meeting standards, and anxious about hidden criticism. Over time, this ambiguity fuelled self-doubt and chipped away at her confidence.

Eventually, after weeks of mounting anxiety, Talia advocated for herself and asked if feedback could be structured differently. She suggested bullet-pointed notes, sent via email a few days before each 1:1. This gave her time to process the information, reflect on her work, and prepare questions in advance.

Her manager agreed, and the change had an immediate impact.

Instead of walking into meetings with dread, Talia came prepared and confident. She knew what was going well, what needed improvement, and how to act on it. Her engagement grew, her performance improved, and the 1:1s became a genuinely useful space for growth.

The lesson here is simple: what made the difference wasn't "fixing" Talia with soft skills training or resilience workshops. It was her manager adjusting how feedback was delivered.

Small Shifts That Make a Big Impact

Here are a few inclusive communication practices that can transform your interactions:

- **Be clear and direct** - avoid idioms, euphemisms or vague requests
- **Check for understanding** - not to test, but to ensure mutual clarity
- **Offer written follow-ups** - especially after meetings or verbal instructions
- **Be open to different processing speeds** - some of us need time to think before speaking
- **Give feedback early and specifically** - and ask how we prefer to receive it
- **Avoid the "just say something" culture** - instead, build trust and ask thoughtful questions

None of this is about lowering expectations. It's about offering the right scaffolding so we can meet them.

Reflection Questions

1. How do I currently communicate with my team, and is that communication style equally accessible to everyone?
2. Have I ever misunderstood an autistic employee because they communicated differently to what I expected?
3. What assumptions do I make based on tone, body language or silence?
4. Do I provide clear written feedback, expectations or summaries? If not, what's one small change I could implement this week?
5. Have I created space for my autistic team members to share how they prefer to communicate, and have I truly listened?

5

Reasonable Adjustments

What They Are, Why They Matter and How They Transform Workplaces

Dear Manager,

Let's get real about something that can feel complicated but is absolutely vital: reasonable adjustments.

If you're new to this term, or even if you've heard it before, you might think of "adjustments" as a box to tick; something HR requires when someone discloses a disability. But from where I stand, as an autistic employee and advocate, reasonable adjustments are not a favour or a concession. They're a basic necessity. And when done well, they don't just help autistic employees: they improve the workplace for everyone.

What Are Reasonable Adjustments and Why Do They Matter?

The term "reasonable adjustments" comes from the Equality Act 2010 in Great Britain, which mandates that employers must take appropriate steps to remove or reduce disadvantages faced by disabled employees.

Put simply, reasonable adjustments are changes or adaptations to the work environment, processes or expectations that help an employee facing negative long-term effects perform their job effectively.

The law doesn't list every adjustment you must make. Instead, it says the adjustments must be reasonable, meaning practical and proportional given the size and resources of the organisation.

But "reasonable" is a flexible concept. What's reasonable for a multinational might look very different for a small charity. The key is openness, dialogue and a willingness to listen and act.

Research by the Chartered Institute of Personnel and Development (CIPD, 2022) found that 89% of employees with reasonable adjustments in place reported improved productivity and wellbeing. Conversely, the absence of adjustments can lead to increased absenteeism, poor mental health and ultimately losing talented staff.

For autistic employees like me, adjustments can be the difference between surviving and thriving.

Common Misconceptions About Adjustments

I've heard so many managers say, "But Mahlia, I don't know what adjustments you need."

I get it. Adjustments can seem daunting if you've never done them before. But here's the truth: many adjustments are low or no cost, and simple to implement. It's about having a flexible mindset, not money.

For example, allowing me to work with headphones or giving me clear, written instructions costs almost nothing but makes a huge difference.

Examples of Reasonable Adjustments for Autistic Employees

Every person's needs are unique, but here are some of the most commonly effective adjustments I and other autistic professionals have found helpful:

- Flexible working hours to avoid sensory overload during commute or peak office times
- Quiet or low-stimulation workspaces away from noisy, bright or open-plan offices
- Written summaries or agendas before meetings to allow processing time
- Clear, direct communication without euphemisms or idioms
- Breaks during the day to manage sensory or emotional overwhelm
- Use of technology or alternative tools to support organisation or time management
- Adjusted performance metrics that consider neurodivergent working styles

My Personal Example: The Power of Simple Adjustments

I remember early in my career, I was placed in a bustling open-plan office. The constant noise and bright lights were overwhelming. I tried to push through, but my productivity plummeted, and I became anxious and exhausted.

When I eventually disclosed my autism, the company arranged for me to work remotely two days a week and provided a desk in a quieter part of the office on the other days.

That simple adjustment changed everything. My focus improved, my anxiety decreased, and I felt valued, not just tolerated.

Case Study: Reasonable Adjustments in Action

Ethan, a talented software developer, excelled technically but struggled with the team's daily stand-up meetings. These were short, rapid-fire sessions where everyone was expected to share quick updates. The noisy, fast-paced environment left Ethan overwhelmed, and they often left the meetings unsure about their tasks. Their manager misinterpreted this as a lack of engagement or even disinterest - a classic example of poor management, where behaviours were judged without considering the impact of the environment.

The turning point came after Ethan disclosed their autism. Instead of dismissing their concerns, Ethan's manager chose to listen and collaborate. Together, they identified small but powerful adjustments that transformed the experience:

- The agenda was shared in advance so Ethan could prepare.
- They were given the option to submit updates in writing before the meeting, reducing the pressure to think and speak at speed.
- The meeting location was moved to a quieter room with fewer distractions.

These were not costly changes, but they made a world of difference. Ethan's confidence and participation grew, their updates became clearer, and their contributions were better recognised by the team. The manager also reported a noticeable boost in team cohesion and overall productivity - proof that when managers adapt processes, the benefits ripple outward. This recognises that reasonable adjustments often improve working life for the whole team.

How to Approach Reasonable Adjustments

1. Start with an open conversation, invite your employee to share what works for them without pressure or judgment.
2. Remember that adjustments are likely to be a trial and error; what works at one time might need tweaking later. Flexibility is key, as is maintaining this mindset.
3. Document agreed adjustments, so there's clarity and accountability for everyone involved.
4. Review adjustments regularly; people's needs can change, especially in dynamic roles or environments.
5. Encourage a culture where asking for adjustments is normalised and not stigmatised.

The Role of Intersectionality in Adjustments

Intersectionality is a framework coined by Kimberlé Crenshaw that recognises how multiple aspects of identity (race, gender, disability, class, etc.) intersect to affect experiences of discrimination or privilege.

An autistic employee from a marginalised ethnic background may face layered challenges that affect what adjustments are needed or how comfortable they feel disclosing their needs.

For example, they might fear stigma in both their cultural community and the workplace, so sensitive, confidential conversations are critical.

Further insights into how intersectionality shapes effective workplace adjustments are explored in Chapter 8.

Why You Should See Reasonable Adjustments as an Investment

Making reasonable adjustments isn't just a legal requirement or "nice to have", it's a smart investment. A 2020 report by Deloitte found that inclusive workplaces experience up to 30% higher innovation revenue and 25% lower turnover.

By supporting your autistic employees with the right adjustments, you're unlocking potential, reducing absenteeism and building loyalty.

As a manager, you have the power to transform someone's work life entirely with something as simple as a small change in environment, communication or schedule.

Reasonable adjustments are not burdensome; they are bridges, bridges to inclusion, to respect, to better performance.

Remember, adjustments are as individual as the person requesting them. What feels reasonable is a conversation, not a checklist.

Reflection Questions

1. What reasonable adjustments do I currently offer, and how do I learn about the needs of autistic employees without assumptions?
2. Have I created a safe space where employees feel comfortable discussing and bringing up adjustments?
3. What small, low-cost adjustments could I trial with autistic employees to support their success?
4. How often do I review and adapt adjustments to ensure they remain effective?
5. Am I considering the diverse identities and lived experiences of my autistic employees when discussing adjustments?

6

Supporting Sensory Needs and Reducing Overwhelm

How Understanding Sensory Processing Can Unlock Autistic Potential at Work

Dear Manager,

I want to take a moment to talk about something that is often overlooked but is absolutely fundamental for many autistic people like me: sensory needs.

For years, I didn't understand why the office environment was so exhausting. Why the flicker of fluorescent lights made me want to shut my eyes. Why background noise sometimes felt like a physical attack. Why a sudden touch on the shoulder would send me into panic.

I was told I was "too sensitive" or that I needed to "not be so jumpy." But what I was experiencing was sensory overwhelm, and it's a very real, very valid part of how my autistic brain processes the world.

In this chapter, I want to share what sensory processing means, how it affects autistic employees and what practical steps you can take to reduce overwhelm in your workplace.

What Is Sensory Processing?

Sensory processing refers to how our brains receive, interpret and respond to sensory information, like sights, sounds, smells, touch, tastes and even internal bodily sensations.

For autistic people, sensory processing can be atypical, meaning:

- We may experience hypersensitivity (over-responsiveness), where stimuli feel overwhelming or painful
- Or hyposensitivity (under-responsiveness), where stimuli might barely register, causing us to seek more input
- Sometimes, it's a mix of both, depending on the sense or context

This isn't about being "picky" or "needy"; it's a neurological reality. Sensory overwhelm can trigger fight, flight or freeze responses, leading to anxiety, shutdowns or meltdowns.

Quick Definitions:

- Sensory Overload: When the brain receives more sensory input than it can manage, leading to distress or shutdown.
- Stimming: Repetitive movements or sounds that help regulate sensory input and emotions (e.g., rocking, hand-flapping).
- Shutdown: A state of becoming non-responsive due to overwhelm, often mistaken for withdrawal or defiance.
- Meltdown: An intense response to sensory or emotional overload, which can look like an outburst but is not controlled behaviour.

Why Sensory Needs Matter at Work

The modern workplace often seems designed to maximise sensory input rather than minimise it. Think bright fluorescent lighting, noisy open-plan offices, background chatter, unpredictable interruptions, strong scents from cleaning products, perfumes and food.

For many autistic employees, this environment is like being on constant alert. It depletes our energy, makes concentration difficult and can impact our mental health.

Research from the National Autistic Society (2020) found that over 60% of autistic adults identify sensory issues as a significant workplace challenge. Sensory overwhelm is linked to higher rates of anxiety, depression and burnout.

But here's the good news: by understanding and adapting the sensory environment, you can reduce overwhelm and unlock potential.

My Experience: The Battle with Overhead Lights

I remember working in an office where the overhead lights flickered faintly. No one else seemed to notice. But for me, the flicker felt like a strobe, causing headaches and eye strain.

I tried wearing sunglasses indoors, which wasn't always possible, or avoiding eye contact to reduce discomfort. I masked my irritation because I didn't want to appear difficult.

Eventually, I disclosed my sensory sensitivity. My employer replaced the lights with two light switches, so we only had to use half the lights in the office, and had the flicker fixed. That simple change improved my focus and wellbeing dramatically.

Practical Ways to Support Sensory Needs

Here are some concrete steps you can take to reduce sensory overwhelm for autistic employees:

1. Create Quiet Spaces

Allow access to quiet rooms or areas where noise and distractions are minimised. This is essential for recharge and focus.

2. Offer Flexible Work Options

Remote or hybrid working can allow employees to control their sensory environment. Flexible hours can also help avoid overwhelming commutes.

3. Adjust Lighting

Switch to natural or adjustable lighting where possible. Offer desk lamps or the option to wear tinted sunglasses.

4. Manage Noise Levels

Provide noise-cancelling headphones or earplugs. Use "quiet hours" or "no meeting days" to reduce background noise.

5. Be Mindful of Smells

Avoid strong perfumes, air fresheners or cleaning products in shared spaces.

6. Allow Breaks

Encourage regular breaks for sensory regulation. These can be short walks, quiet moments or stimming breaks.

7. Educate the Team

Raise awareness about sensory differences to build empathy and reduce accidental overwhelm (like unexpected loud noises or touch).

Case Study: Sensory Adjustments in Practice

Alex, a software engineer in a busy tech company, was struggling with the open office environment. His desk was positioned near a high-traffic corridor, and the constant footsteps, candescent lighting, and background chatter drained his energy every day. Before long, he was on the verge of quitting - a clear sign that the workplace setup was becoming unsustainable.

At first, Alex's manager didn't notice the problem. The signs of overwhelm (fatigue, withdrawal, and dips in focus) were misread as a lack of motivation. This was poor practice: assuming the issue lay with the employee's attitude, rather than pausing to consider the role of other factors.

Everything shifted after Alex disclosed his autism. Instead of brushing it off, his manager chose to listen and act. Together, they made a few simple adjustments: Alex moved to a quieter corner, noise-cancelling headphones were provided, and he was given the option to work remotely twice a week.

The impact was immediate. Alex's productivity increased, his stress levels dropped, and his job satisfaction returned. His manager later reflected, *"We didn't realise how much sensory factors affected him until we asked and had the conversations."* This was good management in action: recognising the power of open dialogue and making reasonable adjustments that benefitted both Alex and the wider team.

The Ripple Effect: Sensory-Friendly Workplaces Help Everyone

Not every autistic person experiences sensory input the same way. Some may seek certain sensory stimulations, like tactile objects or movement breaks, while others need avoidance.

This is why listening and collaborating with each employee is vital. Don't guess what someone needs based on assumptions or stereotypes.

Creating sensory-friendly spaces benefits not only autistic employees but also those with anxiety, migraines, PTSD or even neurotypical colleagues who want a calm environment.

Reflection Questions

1. How does the physical environment of my workplace impact sensory processing for autistic employees?
2. Have I created or advocated for quiet, low-stimulation spaces?
3. How do I currently accommodate sensory needs in team routines and environments?
4. Am I aware of the sensory triggers common in my workplace (e.g., lighting, noise, smells)?
5. How can I encourage open dialogue about sensory needs with employees without pressuring disclosure?

7

Flexible Working and Routine Adaptations

Why Flexibility Isn't a Perk; It's a Necessity for Autistic Employees

Dear Manager,

If there's one truth I've learned navigating workplaces as an autistic person, it's this: routine is safety and flexibility is freedom.

Many of us rely on predictable routines to feel grounded and reduce anxiety. Change, especially sudden or unexplained change, can be a huge source of stress. But rigid, inflexible work environments can make this worse, pushing autistic employees to the edge.

In this chapter, I want to share why flexible working arrangements and thoughtful routine adaptations are vital, not just for wellbeing, but for unlocking autistic potential and long-term retention.

Why Routine Matters So Much

Routine is more than habit. For autistic people, it's a cognitive anchor. It reduces uncertainty, eases sensory overwhelm, and helps manage executive functioning challenges like planning and prioritising.

Sudden changes in daily tasks, meeting times or workplace location can dislodge this anchor, leading to stress, reduced focus or shutdown.

A 2022 survey by the Autistica charity showed that over 75% of autistic adults reported anxiety linked to unpredictable workplace routines.

But Flexibility Is Just as Crucial

Paradoxically, while routine offers comfort, flexibility allows us to adapt to our needs and prevent overwhelm.

For example, working from home may reduce sensory stressors, but might make it harder to structure the day without routine. Flexibility means balancing these factors.

Research from Frontiers in Psychology (2023) highlights that autistic employees thrive best when they have control over both their routines and the flexibility to adapt them as needed.

My Experience: Finding Balance Through Flexibility

At one point in my career, I was tied to rigid office hours: 9 to 5, in person. I struggled with the sensory noise of commuting and the unpredictable meetings that broke up my focus.

When my employer allowed me to shift my hours and work remotely two days a week, my stress levels dropped dramatically.

I could design my day to match my natural energy rhythms, take breaks when overwhelmed and prepare better for meetings.

That flexibility made me feel trusted and respected. I didn't just survive; I began to bloom.

Practical Ways to Support Flexible Working and Routine Adaptations

Here are some effective strategies you can implement:

1. Offer Flexible Hours

Allow employees to start and finish work at times that suit their energy levels and reduce stressful commutes. This also considers split shifts.

2. Remote or Hybrid Working Options

Provide opportunities to work from home or quieter environments when needed.

3. Predictable Schedules

Where possible, fix meeting times, deadlines and routines well in advance to minimise surprises.

4. Notice of Changes

Give as much advance notice as possible when routines or schedules change. If possible, give context to these changes.

5. Structured Agendas and Calendars

Provide clear, detailed agendas before meetings and regular calendar updates.

6. Task Breakdown and Prioritisation

Help autistic employees structure their work by breaking down large projects into manageable steps.

7. Allow "Buffer Time"

Encourage breaks between meetings or tasks to prevent sensory or cognitive overload.

Case Study: Routine Adaptation in Practice

Rhea, an autistic project manager, was exceptionally strong in her role. Her gift for detailed planning, risk mapping, and forward-thinking made her a real asset to the team. But she struggled when meetings were rescheduled at short notice. For her, last-minute changes disrupted her carefully structured workflow and created spirals of stress and anxiety.

At first, her manager didn't recognise the problem. When Rhea became visibly tense or frustrated after a change, it was put down to her being "rigid" or "inflexible". Instead of asking what was behind the stress, the manager framed Rhea's reaction as a personal flaw rather than seeing the very real impact of unpredictability on her ability to function at her best.

Things improved once her manager took the time to listen. Through a constructive conversation, it became clear that what Rhea needed wasn't to be more "flexible", but for her environment to be more predictable. Her manager responded by introducing a "no last-minute changes" policy for meetings involving Rhea, and by sharing a weekly planner with fixed deadlines and clear timelines. These small but intentional adjustments made all the difference.

With more certainty in her schedule, Rhea's stress levels reduced. She felt empowered and in control, which not only improved her project delivery, but also boosted collaboration across the whole team. The manager, too, noticed that meetings became more focused and deadlines were met more consistently, demonstrating that what's good for autistic employees often benefits everyone.

The Role of Technology

Technology can be a powerful ally. Tools like calendar apps with reminders, task management software and communication platforms with threaded conversations can help autistic employees maintain structure and predictability.

Encouraging the use of these tools and being flexible in allowing their use can boost autonomy and productivity.

Intersectionality and Flexibility

Remember, intersectionality means that employees' experiences of flexibility and routine needs may be influenced by other identities such as disability, gender or caregiving responsibilities.

For example, a single parent who is autistic might need flexibility not only for sensory reasons, but also to manage childcare.

Being aware of these layered needs helps create truly inclusive workplaces.

Flexibility and routine aren't opposing forces; they're two sides of the same coin. When balanced thoughtfully, they create a supportive environment where autistic employees can contribute their best work.

Your willingness to adapt routines and offer flexibility sends a powerful message: we see you. We respect your needs. We want you here for the long haul.

Reflection Questions

1. How rigid or flexible are the current work routines in my team or organisation?
2. What steps do I take to provide advance notice for schedule changes?
3. How can I involve autistic employees in designing routines that

work for them?

4. What technologies or tools can support routine and flexibility?

8

Supporting Diverse Autistic Employees

Why Seeing The Whole Person Matters

Dear Manager,

One of the most important lessons I've learned on my journey is that autism is not a single story.

Just like any group, autistic people are incredibly diverse. We come from different races, genders, sexual orientations, socio-economic backgrounds and cultures. Each of these identities shapes how we experience the world, including the workplace.

This is where the concept of intersectionality comes in.

What Is Intersectionality?

Intersectionality is a term coined by legal scholar Kimberlé Crenshaw in 1989 to describe how different aspects of identity, intersect and overlap, creating unique experiences of discrimination or privilege.

In other words, someone isn't just autistic, they might also be a woman, a person of colour, LGBTQ+ or a caregiver. These overlapping identities affect how they experience workplace inclusion or exclusion.

Why Intersectionality Matters for Autism in the Workplace

Many diversity and inclusion efforts focus on one identity at a time. But for autistic employees, especially those with multiple marginalised identities, the experience is more complex.

For example:

- A Black autistic woman might face racial bias alongside stereotypes about her autism, creating compounded barriers.
- An autistic transgender person might experience misunderstanding about both their neurodivergence and gender identity.
- Undiagnosed autistic employees from lower socio-economic backgrounds may lack access to diagnosis or workplace resources.

Research from Autistica and The National Autistic Society (2022) highlights that autistic people from marginalised groups often report worse employment outcomes and greater workplace discrimination.

My Experience: Navigating Multiple Identities

As an autistic woman of colour, my experiences in the workplace extend far beyond autism alone. I do not move through the world, or the workplace, in the same way a white autistic man might. Too often, I've been stereotyped as "emotional" or "difficult," labels that are both gendered and racialised. At times, colleagues have misinterpreted my communication style not only through the lens of autism, but also through unconscious racial and gender biases.

Being called "emotional" for speaking up, or "difficult" for asserting myself, reflects broader stereotypes that many women and people of colour face. When these biases intersect with assumptions about autism, the barriers to genuine workplace inclusion only deepen.

This is why understanding intersectionality, the way different aspects of our identity overlap and shape our experiences, is vital. None of us live in just one identity box. True inclusion requires acknowledging the whole person, not only a single part of who they are.

Supporting Diverse Autistic Employees: What You Can Do

1. **Listen and Learn** Create safe spaces for autistic employees to share their whole selves. Don't assume autism is the only identity shaping their experience.
2. **Challenge Stereotypes and Biases** Be aware of how unconscious biases about race, gender and other identities can affect perceptions of autistic employees.
3. **Tailor Adjustments and Support** Recognise that a "one-size-fits-all" approach won't work. Adjustments may need to reflect the complexity of intersecting identities.
4. **Promote Diverse Role Models** Representation matters. Highlight diverse autistic voices and leadership to inspire and normalise difference.
5. **Collaborate with Intersectional Employee Networks** Support or establish networks that address multiple identities, such as neurodiversity and ethnicity or LGBTQ+ groups.

Case Study: Intersectionality in Action

Samira, a queer autistic woman from a refugee background, faced multiple barriers in her workplace. It wasn't just her autism that shaped her experience - language differences, cultural misunderstandings and biases around gender and sexuality also affected how colleagues perceived and interacted with her. For example, in team meetings, when Samira paused to find the right words, some colleagues assumed she didn't have strong ideas to contribute. Others misinterpreted her direct communication style as abrupt or unfriendly. Her manager at first overlooked these issues, viewing them as "personality clashes" rather than recognising them as signs of deeper systemic barriers. This was poor management: minimising her struggles instead of acknowledging the complex intersection of factors at play.

Things changed when her manager chose to take a more inclusive and curious approach. Instead of expecting Samira to adapt to a workplace culture that wasn't designed for her, the manager invested time in learning about the multiple facets of her identity and how these shaped her workplace experience. Together, they co-created a culturally sensitive, neuroinclusive support plan. This included:

- Flexible communication methods, allowing Samira to prepare written input for meetings alongside verbal contributions.
- A mentoring arrangement with a trusted senior colleague who shared aspects of her lived experience.
- Opportunities for cultural awareness training across the wider team, to reduce misunderstandings and foster empathy.

The impact was clear. Samira began to feel valued for her insights rather than judged for her differences. Her confidence grew, and she was able to contribute fully to projects, bringing perspectives that enriched the team's work. Her manager, too, noticed improvements in collaboration and team morale once the adjustments were in place.

By embracing intersectionality, workplaces don't just help autistic employees; they build cultures that respect and celebrate all forms of diversity. This leads to greater creativity, employee wellbeing and overall organisational success.

Reflection Questions

1. How am I currently acknowledging the multiple identities of autistic employees in my team?
2. What unconscious biases might I hold that affect my perception of autistic employees with diverse backgrounds?
3. How can I create safer spaces for sharing and learning about intersectional experiences?
4. What steps can I take to ensure that support and adjustments are personalised and holistic?
5. Are there employee networks or resources I can connect with to better support intersectional inclusion?

9

Encouraging Self-Advocacy and Open Dialogue

Empowering Autistic Employees to Find Their Voice and Fostering Trust

Dear Manager,

One of the most profound shifts in my journey as an autistic professional has been learning to self-advocate; to speak up for my needs, respect my boundaries and recognise my strengths.

But self-advocacy doesn't happen in a vacuum. It requires a workplace culture where open dialogue is safe, encouraged and respected.

In this chapter, I want to share why fostering self-advocacy matters, how you can support it as a manager, and how open communication builds bridges of trust that benefit everyone.

What Is Self-Advocacy?

Self-advocacy means understanding and expressing your own needs, rights and desires in a way that helps you access support and participate fully.

For autistic people, this can be a steep learning curve. Many of us have been conditioned to mask, suppress or minimise our needs to fit in. Years of being misunderstood or dismissed can make speaking up daunting.

Research from The National Autistic Society (2021) found that autistic employees who felt confident to self-advocate were three times more likely to report job satisfaction and wellbeing.

Managers hold a unique role as gatekeepers to resources, adjustments and workplace culture.

Your willingness to listen without judgment, validate experiences and respond constructively can encourage autistic employees to voice their needs early, preventing burnout and disengagement.

My Experience: Finding My Voice

Early in my career, I rarely spoke up about the challenges I faced. I feared negative consequences, being seen as "difficult" or being worried about jeopardising my job.

It wasn't until a manager explicitly invited me to share my experiences and preferences that I began to feel safe.

That conversation was transformational as it opened doors for adjustments that improved my work and wellbeing; it showed me that my voice mattered.

Creating Open Dialogue: Practical Tips

1. **Regular Check-ins** Schedule one-to-one meetings with autistic employees to invite feedback, questions or concerns in a relaxed setting.
2. **Normalise Disclosure** Communicate clearly that sharing diagnosis or support needs is voluntary and respected.
3. **Active Listening** Show empathy by reflecting back what you hear, asking clarifying questions and avoiding premature solutions or dismissal.
4. **Encourage Written Communication** Some autistic people find it easier to express themselves in writing. Offer multiple channels for communication.
5. **Co-create Solutions** When needs arise, involve employees in developing adjustments or strategies rather than imposing solutions.

Case Study: Sam's Journey to Self-Advocacy

Sam, a talented graphic designer, began their role feeling overwhelmed and isolated. They struggled to ask for adjustments, partly due to fear that their needs would be dismissed or judged negatively. In the early days, their manager missed several signs of their distress, such as Sam's hesitancy in meetings and frequent after-hours working, assuming they were "quiet" or simply adjusting slowly. This was poor conduct: overlooking potential barriers and failing to create proactive opportunities for discussion.

The situation improved when their manager took a different approach. Instead of waiting for Sam to speak up, she initiated confidential monthly check-ins. She asked open, non-judgmental questions like: *"Is there anything you'd like me to know?"* and *"Is there a way I can support you better?"* This shift in practice created trust and signalled to Sam that it was safe to share.

Gradually, Sam disclosed their sensory sensitivities, such as difficulty concentrating in noisy open spaces, and their preference for written over verbal instructions. Working together, they and their manager co-created a personalised support plan. This included clearer task briefs, quieter spaces for focused work, and flexibility around their schedule.

The results were striking: Sam's confidence grew, their productivity improved, and they began contributing more visibly to the creative process. What started as a journey of hesitancy turned into one of empowerment, simply because their manager moved from reactive assumptions to proactive listening and collaboration.

Why Open Dialogue Benefits the Whole Team

When employees feel safe to speak openly, it leads to:

- Better problem-solving
- Reduced misunderstandings
- Increased trust and engagement
- Stronger team cohesion

Reflection Questions

1. How do I currently invite feedback and communication from autistic employees?
2. Do I provide multiple ways for employees to express their needs?
3. How comfortable do autistic employees in my team feel about disclosing and self-advocating?
4. How can I improve my active listening skills to better support open dialogue?
5. What steps can I take to co-create solutions rather than dictate

adjustments?

10

Supporting Growth and Performance Compassionately

How to Nurture Potential Without Pressure

Dear Manager,

Supporting an autistic employee's growth and performance can feel like walking a tightrope. You want to encourage development and success, but without pushing so hard that it triggers overwhelm or burnout.

This chapter is about striking that balance; creating a compassionate environment where autistic employees can grow confidently and authentically, with support tailored to their needs.

Why Compassionate Performance Support Matters

Traditional performance management often assumes a one-size-fits-all approach: regular reviews, targets and sometimes harsh feedback. For autistic employees, this can be daunting.

A 2022 report by the Harvard Business Review emphasises that workplaces adopting compassionate performance practices see a 20% increase in employee retention and engagement, particularly among neurodivergent staff.

Compassionate support recognises individual differences, encourages strengths and addresses challenges with kindness rather than criticism.

Defining Compassionate Performance Management

At its core, it means:

- Focusing on strengths and potential rather than deficits
- Setting clear, realistic expectations collaboratively
- Providing consistent, constructive feedback in a respectful way
- Allowing flexibility in how goals are achieved
- Supporting wellbeing alongside productivity

My Experience: When Feedback Felt Like Failure

In my career, I recall a performance review where my manager's feedback was vague and framed negatively: "You need to be more proactive."

I left feeling confused and demoralised because I didn't know what "more proactive" meant in practice, nor how to improve.

Later, I worked with a manager who approached feedback differently; she gave specific examples, highlighted my strengths and invited me to co-create improvement goals.

That shift changed everything. I felt supported, motivated and clear about my path forward.

Practical Steps to Support Growth Compassionately

1. **Set Clear, Specific Goals** Avoid vague terms. For example, instead of "be more proactive" try "take the lead on project X by providing weekly updates."
2. **Focus on Strengths** Identify and build on what the employee does well. This boosts confidence and engagement.
3. **Provide Regular, Timely Feedback** Don't wait for annual reviews. Frequent, low-key check-ins help adjust support dynamically.
4. **Tailor Feedback Style** Ask how the employee prefers to receive feedback: written, verbal, or with examples.
5. **Celebrate Small Wins** Acknowledging progress, no matter how small, nurtures motivation and wellbeing.
6. **Integrate Wellbeing Support** Recognise that mental health impacts performance. Connect employees with resources or reasonable adjustments as needed.

Case Study: A Compassionate Growth Plan in Action

Kamal, a bright marketing analyst, often struggled to meet deadlines. The challenge wasn't a lack of skill or effort - it stemmed from executive functioning difficulties, which are common in autism and affect planning, prioritising and managing multiple tasks at once.

At first, Kamal's manager misread the situation. Missed deadlines were interpreted as disorganisation or even a lack of commitment. This was poor management: focusing on outcomes without exploring the underlying reasons. The response was to apply more pressure, which only heightened Kamal's stress and led to further delays. Instead of motivating him, the pressure created a cycle of anxiety and underperformance.

The turning point came when his manager chose a more sympathetic approach. In a supportive one-to-one, she asked open questions and listened carefully to Kamal's experiences. Together, they co-designed a growth plan that worked with Kamal's strengths instead of against his challenges. The plan included:

- Breaking large projects into smaller, more manageable steps
- Agreeing on realistic timelines for each stage of work
- Using project management software to track progress visually
- Providing weekly feedback that highlighted completed tasks first, before moving on to what was still pending

These adjustments transformed Kamal's experience. Instead of feeling overwhelmed, he now had clarity and structure. Weekly feedback helped him focus on progress rather than on what he hadn't yet achieved. His output steadily improved, his confidence grew, and his anxiety about deadlines reduced significantly. Over time, he even began mentoring new team members, sharing tips he had learned along the way.

Supporting Career Development

Remember, autistic employees have ambitions, talents and career goals like anyone else. Supporting their development might include:

- Providing mentorship or coaching
- Offering training opportunities tailored to learning styles
- Supporting transitions into new roles gradually
- Recognising and accommodating social or sensory challenges in networking or team-building events
- Acknowledging and providing alternatives to managerial positions

Reflection Questions

1. How do I currently deliver feedback to autistic employees? Is it clear, specific and compassionate?
2. Do I regularly check in to adjust support based on the employee's experiences and needs?
3. How can I better recognise and build on the strengths of autistic team members?
4. What career development opportunities am I offering that are accessible and inclusive?
5. How do I integrate wellbeing support with performance management?

11

Building Awareness and Neuroinclusion Across Your Team

Creating a Culture Where Everyone Understands and Values Neurodiversity

Dear Manager,

Supporting autistic employees effectively isn't just about individual adjustments, it's about building a workplace culture where neurodiversity is understood, respected and celebrated.

This concept, neuroinclusion, means creating environments where neurological differences, like autism, ADHD, dyslexia and others, are not just accommodated, but embraced as strengths.

In this chapter, I want to share why team-wide awareness matters, how to foster neuroinclusion and what you can do to cultivate empathy and understanding in your workplace.

What Is Neuroinclusion and Why Build Awareness?

Neuroinclusion refers to the intentional effort to include and support neurodivergent individuals fully within an organisation.

It goes beyond compliance with legal requirements or individual accommodations. It's about changing attitudes, policies and practices to ensure neurodivergent people feel valued and empowered.

Many of the challenges autistic employees face come from misunderstandings, stereotypes and stigma.

A study by The Centre for Neurodiversity (2023) showed that workplaces with neurodiversity training reported 40% higher retention rates of autistic employees.

When colleagues understand autism better, they're more patient, supportive and collaborative.

Common Myths About Autism to Challenge

- **Myth: Autistic people lack empathy** In reality, many autistic individuals experience empathy differently, often deeply feeling others' emotions but struggling to express it conventionally.
- **Myth: Autism means being anti-social or uninterested in relationships** Many autistic people value connection deeply but may communicate or socialise differently.
- **Myth: Autism is a deficit only condition** Autism brings many strengths, for instance, unique perspectives, attention to detail and creativity.

Challenging these myths helps create a culture of respect.

My Experience: When Awareness Changed Everything

At one point in my career, a team workshop on autism was introduced. Suddenly, colleagues began asking thoughtful questions instead of making assumptions. Small things changed, like more direct communication, patience during sensory overwhelm and celebrating different problem-solving approaches.

That awareness made me feel seen and valued beyond just my role or diagnosis.

How to Build Neuroinclusion in Your Team

1. **Provide Neurodiversity Training** Offer evidence-based training that covers autism basics, sensory needs, communication styles and inclusion strategies.
2. **Encourage Open Conversations** Create forums or safe spaces for sharing experiences and asking questions without judgement.
3. **Lead by Example** Demonstrate inclusive language, empathy and willingness to learn.
4. **Embed Neuroinclusion in Policies** Ensure recruitment, onboarding and performance management reflect neuroinclusive principles.
5. **Celebrate Neurodiversity** Highlight successes of neurodivergent employees and include neurodiversity in diversity and inclusion events.

Case Study: Transforming Culture Through Neuroinclusion

Tara worked with a large financial services company that was facing a troubling trend: high turnover among autistic staff. Exit interviews revealed recurring themes: employees felt misunderstood, unsupported, and pressured to "mask" their differences just to fit in. Managers often viewed difficulties through a deficit lens: if someone seemed withdrawn in meetings, it was assumed they lacked interest; if they requested adjustments, it was quietly seen as "special treatment". The lack of awareness and the stigma surrounding neurodiversity created a culture where talented employees didn't feel safe or valued, leading many to leave.

The company decided to take a different approach. They introduced comprehensive neurodiversity training for managers and staff, tackling myths and equipping people with practical tools to be more inclusive. They also set up a neuroinclusion task force, made up of both neurodivergent and neurotypical employees, to review policies and champion change across the organisation. This shift in culture represented good management: leadership recognised that systemic issues, not individual employees, were the problem.

The results were significant. Within a year, turnover among autistic employees dropped by 35%. More importantly, staff reported feeling "more understood," "safer," and "proud to be themselves." The company didn't just retain talented employees, it also unlocked greater engagement, innovation, and trust across the workforce.

Reflection Questions

1. What neurodiversity training or awareness initiatives does my organisation currently have?
2. How comfortable are team members in discussing neurodiversity openly?
3. How do I model inclusive language and behaviours?
4. Are our policies reflective of neuroinclusion principles?
5. How can I celebrate neurodiversity more visibly in my team?

12

Handling Disclosure and Confidentiality Respectfully

Creating a Safe Space for Trust and Authenticity

Dear Manager,

Disclosure: the decision to share an autism diagnosis or neurodivergent status with an employer. This is one of the most personal and complex experiences autistic employees face.

For me, and many others, deciding whether, when and how to disclose has felt like skating on thin ice. There's hope for understanding and support, but also fear of stigma, discrimination or breaches of privacy.

How you, as a manager or HR professional, handle disclosure and confidentiality can shape an autistic employee's sense of safety, belonging and trust.

This chapter explores why respectful handling matters, how to create supportive disclosure processes, and best practices for confidentiality.

What Is Disclosure and Why Does It Matter?

Disclosure means sharing personal information about being autistic with your employer or colleagues. This can be formal or informal, partial or full.

Some autistic people disclose at the hiring stage, others wait until they feel safe, and some never disclose due to fear of negative consequences.

A 2023 survey by The National Autistic Society found that nearly 50% of autistic adults who disclosed at work experienced some form of discrimination or lack of understanding.

Disclosure often opens the door to reasonable adjustments and workplace support. Without it, autistic employees may struggle silently.

However, disclosure is a choice, not a requirement. Employers must respect autonomy and avoid pressuring employees.

Best Practices for Handling Disclosure

1. **Create a Safe Environment** Communicate that disclosure is voluntary and welcome, not mandatory.
2. **Be Clear About Confidentiality** Explain who will know, why and how information will be protected. Always seek explicit consent before sharing.
3. **Train Managers and HR** Ensure they understand the nuances of disclosure and the legal protections around privacy and discrimination.
4. **Offer Multiple Disclosure Channels** Some may prefer to disclose via HR, an occupational health professional or trusted managers.
5. **Follow Up with Support** After disclosure, proactively discuss adjustments and check in regularly.

Case Study: Respecting Confidentiality Builds Trust

Jade, an autistic employee working in a busy corporate environment, chose to disclose her diagnosis to the HR team but asked that her direct manager not be informed right away. For Jade, this boundary was crucial. She wanted time to feel out the workplace culture and decide for herself when, and if, she felt safe to share with her line manager.

In some organisations, a substandard approach would have looked very different. HR might have immediately passed on the information without consent, reasoning that managers "needed to know." This breach of confidentiality could have severely damaged Jade's trust, left her feeling exposed, and reinforced her fear that disclosure would only lead to gossip or discrimination.

Instead, HR took a thoughtful approach. They respected Jade's boundary, working discreetly behind the scenes to implement support measures. Adjustments were made subtly: her hours were made more flexible, and her desk was relocated to a quieter area to reduce sensory overwhelm. None of these changes singled her out, and none undermined her confidentiality.

Because her autonomy was respected, Jade gradually felt safer in her workplace. Over time, she chose to disclose to her manager herself, in her own words and on her own terms. When she did, the conversation was collaborative and positive, and her manager felt prepared to support her thanks to HR's earlier groundwork.

The outcome was twofold: Jade gained the adjustments she needed without compromising her privacy, and her eventual disclosure strengthened trust and collaboration within the team.

Reflection Questions

1. How clear and supportive is my organisation's policy on disclosure and confidentiality?
2. Do I communicate effectively that disclosure is voluntary and respected?
3. How do I ensure confidentiality is maintained consistently?
4. Have I received training on handling disclosure sensitively?
5. How can I create multiple safe disclosure pathways for employees?

13

Conclusion: Leading with Empathy and Inclusion

Dear Manager,

As we reach the final chapter of this book, I want to pause and acknowledge you. You've taken the time to understand, to learn, to reflect and that matters deeply. Creating a workplace where autistic employees can thrive isn't just about policies or checklists. It's about culture. It's about trust. It's about you.

Throughout this guide, I've spoken from my lived experience as an autistic person who has navigated both the wonderful and the overwhelming parts of working life. I've also shared research, stories from others and insights from my work supporting employees on their neuroinclusion journey.

But here's the core truth: autistic employees don't need to be "fixed". We're not broken. We don't need to be "managed" into sameness. What we do need are workplaces that make space for difference, that value our ways of thinking, allow us to work how we work best, and provide the flexibility and support for us to flourish.

The Human Cost of Inaction

Let's be honest. Without active support, many autistic people burn out. We mask. We overcompensate. We fall through the cracks. A study published in Autism journal (2022) found that 93% of autistic adults had experienced burnout, often related to masking and a lack of accommodations in the workplace.

Meanwhile, autistic unemployment remains shockingly high. In the UK, just 29% of autistic adults are in any form of employment (ONS, 2021), making us the most underemployed of all disabled groups. And yet, when supported appropriately, autistic employees excel, bringing creativity, integrity, focus and innovation to our roles.

This isn't just a moral imperative. It's also good business.

Changing the Culture: It Starts with You

Real change begins with leaders. With line managers. With HR professionals. With people like you.

When you choose to listen, not just to this book, but to your autistic colleagues, you start to transform not only individual experiences, but the entire workplace culture.

Real Inclusion Isn't One-Size-Fits-All

You might be thinking, "I want to get this right, but I'm afraid I'll say the wrong thing." I hear that a lot. Here's what I want you to know: you don't need to be perfect. You just need to be open.

Ask rather than assume. Create space rather than pressure. Offer options rather than ultimatums. And remember that autistic doesn't mean identical. Each autistic person is unique. For example:

- I work well in flexible, creative work environments with lots of solo time, but others may prefer clear structure and routine.
- I benefit from visual planners and creative rest, yet others might need time-blocking and predictability.
- I find face-to-face meetings draining, but others might find them grounding.

Autism is a spectrum, yes, but not a linear one. Think of it as a constellation of needs, strengths and experiences. That's why co-production (designing support with the employee, not just for them) is so important.

Moving Beyond Inclusion Towards Belonging

It's not enough to include autistic people at the table if we don't feel safe to speak.

Belonging is that deeper level of inclusion where someone knows they're not just tolerated, but valued. Where they don't have to mask or fit into a neurotypical mould just to get by. Where they can show up, as they are, and succeed.

The future of work must be neuroinclusive. And you, Dear Manager, are already helping to shape it.

If You Only Remember One Thing...

Let it be this:

Support doesn't have to be complicated. It has to be compassionate.

Small changes can have life-changing impact.

A dimmed light. A quiet room. An agenda ahead of time. A pause between questions. The offer of remote working. The freedom to stim, to rest, to be.

These may seem minor, but to an autistic employee, they can be the difference between surviving and thriving.

My Hopes for the Future

I dream of workplaces where autistic people don't just "make do" but feel deeply seen and supported.

Where autistic graduates aren't dismissed at the application stage because their social skills don't match narrow expectations.

Where autistic managers are praised for their directness, not penalised for not making small talk.

Where autistic creatives, developers, teachers, engineers, all of us, can do the work we love without masking who we are.

Final Reflection Questions

1. What beliefs about autism in the workplace have shifted for me through this book?
2. What is one action I will take this week to better support an autistic employee?
3. How can I centre the voices of autistic people in future decisions or policies?
4. What ongoing learning (e.g., training, reading, discussion) can I commit to?
5. How can I help create not just neuroinclusion, but true belonging?

A Final Word from Me

Thank you. Thank you for reading. For reflecting. For being willing to walk this path with openness and humility.

It's not always easy to challenge the status quo. But it's worth it.

Because every autistic person deserves a workplace where they can show up fully and prosper.

You're helping to build that world: one conversation, one accommodation, one moment of empathy at a time.

With gratitude,

Mahlia

Resources and Further Support

Guiding You to Tools, Communities and Knowledge for Sustained Inclusion

Dear Manager,

Supporting autistic employees is a journey: one that requires continual learning, openness and connection to the right resources.

I'm sharing these resources to equip you with trusted organisations, practical tools and helpful networks that can guide you, and your team, toward deeper understanding and effective support.

Whether you are just beginning, or want to deepen your neuroinclusion efforts, these resources are invaluable.

Trusted Organisations to Know

1. The National Autistic Society (NAS)

The leading UK charity for autistic people, providing comprehensive guides on autism in employment, workplace adjustments and legal rights.

Website: autism.org.uk

2. Autistica

A UK-based research charity focusing on autism science, including employment studies and wellbeing. Their evidence-based reports are essential for grounding workplace initiatives in current research.

Website: autistica.org.uk

3. Ambitious about Autism

Focuses on education and employment support, with practical toolkits for employers and young autistic people entering the workforce.

Website: ambitiousaboutautism.org.uk

4. Mind

A mental health charity with specific guidance on neurodiversity and mental health at work, offering practical advice for wellbeing support.

Website: mind.org.uk

5. Scope

A disability equality charity offering resources on inclusive workplaces, accessibility and legal advice.

Website: scope.org.uk

Helpful Toolkits and Guides

- **ACAS's Guide on Neurodiversity at Work** Provides legal context, practical advice and examples of reasonable adjustments. acas.org.uk/neurodiversity
- **The Job Accommodation Network (JAN)** (US-based, but valuable globally) A free resource offering hundreds of accommodation ideas for autistic employees and others. jan.wvu.edu
- **Autistic Self Advocacy Network (ASAN)** Run by autistic people for autistic people, their website offers resources on employment rights and advocacy. autisticadvocacy.org

Technology and Apps That Support Neurodivergent Employees

- **Task and Time Management:** Trello, Asana, Todoist
- **Communication:** Slack, Microsoft Teams with threaded conversations
- **Sensory Supports:** Noise-cancelling headphones, fidget tools apps
- **Mental Health:** Headspace, Calm and other mindfulness apps

Encourage your autistic employees to explore what tools help them best and consider integrating these into team workflows.

Training and Consultancy

If you want to deepen your team's understanding or build neuroinclusive policies, consider working with specialist trainers and consultants. Many autistic-led organisations offer bespoke workshops.

My Blog and Personal Work

Of course, I warmly recommend my own blog at mahliaamatina.com/workplace-blog, where I share insights, personal reflections and practical advice for neuroinclusive workplaces.

Building Connections

Consider joining or creating a support network focused on neurodiversity, autism or disability inclusion. These groups provide peer support, raise awareness and inform policy.

Reflection Questions

1. Which organisations or resources have I explored to support neuroinclusion?
2. What training opportunities are available or needed for my team?
3. How can I integrate technology to better support autistic employees?
4. What steps can I take to connect with or establish neurodiversity networks at work?
5. How often do I engage in ongoing learning about autism and inclusion?

Bibliography

Acas. (n.d.). *Neurodiversity in the workplace.* Advisory, Conciliation and Arbitration Service. Available at: https://www.acas.org.uk/neurodiversity (Accessed: August 2025).

Ambitious about Autism. (n.d.). *Employ autism toolkit.* Available at: https://www.ambitiousaboutautism.org.uk (Accessed: August 2025).

Autistic Self Advocacy Network (ASAN). (n.d.). *Resources.* Available at: https://autisticadvocacy.org (Accessed: August 2025).

Autistica. (2023). *Employment and wellbeing: Evidence and recommendations.* Autistica Research. Available at: https://www.autistica.org.uk (Accessed: August 2025).

Centre for Neurodiversity. (2023). *The impact of neurodiversity training on workplace retention.* Centre for Neurodiversity Research Report.

Harvard Business Review. (2022). 'Compassionate performance management and its impact on retention', *Harvard Business Review*, 100(3), pp. 45–52.

Headspace. (n.d.). *Mindfulness and meditation app.* Available at: https://www.headspace.com (Accessed: August 2025).

Job Accommodation Network (JAN). (n.d.). *Accommodation ideas for autism spectrum.* West Virginia University. Available at: https://askjan.org (Accessed: August 2025).

Mind. (n.d.). *Mental health at work – supporting neurodiverse employees.* Mind UK. Available at: https://www.mind.org.uk (Accessed: August 2025).

National Autistic Society. (2021). *The Autism Employment Gap.* London:

National Autistic Society. Available at: https://www.autism.org.uk (Accessed: August 2025).

National Autistic Society. (2023). *Workplace experiences of autistic adults*. London: National Autistic Society.

Office for National Statistics. (2021). *Outcomes for disabled people in the UK: 2021*. https://www.ons.gov.uk/peoplepopulationandcommunity/healthandsocialcare/disability/articles/outcomesfordisabledpeopleintheuk/2021 (Accessed: August 2025).

Scope. (n.d.). *Disability equality resources*. Scope UK. Available at: https://www.scope.org.uk (Accessed: August 2025).

Autism journal. (2022). 'Autistic burnout: Causes, impact and recovery', *Autism*, 26(5), pp. 1235–1248.

About the Author

Mahlia Amatina is an award-winning neurodivergent author, artist and advocate, passionate about creativity, inclusion and reimagining the workplace. Diagnosed as autistic in adulthood and named one of the *Top 50 Influential Neurodiverse Women*, by Women Beyond the Box, Mahlia brings both lived experience and professional insight to her work, bridging the gap between theory, research and the day-to-day realities of autistic life.

Join Mahlia's online community and never miss a new project:

You can connect with me on:

- https://www.mahliaamatina.com
- https://www.facebook.com/MahliaAmatina
- https://linktr.ee/MahliaAmatina
- https://www.instagram.com/MahliaAmatina

Also by Mahlia Amatina

If this book spoke to you, please take a moment to leave a review:

- On your reading platform
- On Goodreads, search "Mahlia Amatina" to find her author page
- Directly on Mahlia's website via the contact form

Your feedback helps Mahlia reach more readers and continue advocating for inclusivity within the workplace. Thank you!

Creative Rest: An Artful Toolkit for Autistic Overwhelm

Gentle exercises and heartfelt guidance to help you find peace, clarity and joy through creativity.

In a world that rarely slows down, autistic minds often carry the weight of sensory overload, social pressure and emotional intensity. Rest can feel unreachable or misunderstood. This book invites you to discover a different kind of rest: one that's creative, compassionate and deeply healing.

Through accessible art exercises, reflective journalling prompts and nurturing self-care strategies, *Creative Rest* offers a gentle path back to yourself. Whether you're navigating overwhelm, shutdown or emotional fatigue, this toolkit will help you regulate your feelings, reconnect with your inner world and honour your unique needs with kindness.

There is no "right" way to rest creatively: only your way. This book is your safe space to explore, express and renew at your own pace, reminding you that rest isn't a luxury but a vital act of self-love.

Autistic Burnout and Mental Health at Work

Feeling drained, overwhelmed or on the edge of burnout? For autistic professionals, burnout isn't just stress: it's survival.

In *Autistic Burnout & Mental Health at Work*, Mahlia Amatina combines lived experience, research and practical tools to help you:

Recognise the early signs of autistic burnout

Recover with phased returns, sensory restoration and energy pacing

Request reasonable adjustments and Access to Work support

Build sustainable wellbeing and belonging at work

Whether you're autistic, supporting an autistic colleague or creating an inclusive workplace, this book offers clarity, compassion and strategies you can use right away.

You are not broken. You are worthy of rest, support and a working life that lets you thrive.

The Autistic Employee Workplace Toolkit

Practical Strategies for Thriving at Work - Self-Advocacy, Sensory Overload Management, Reasonable Adjustments and Career Growth for Autistic Professionals.

Thrive as an autistic professional with this practical, empowering guide. Packed with strategies for workplace accommodations, reasonable adjustments, managing sensory overload and self-advocacy, this toolkit helps you navigate autism in the workplace with confidence. Discover how to protect your emotional wellbeing, set clear boundaries, prevent autistic burnout and build a sustainable, fulfilling career.

Autism and Work

Thriving in the Workplace is a supportive, practical guide by autistic artist and advocate Mahlia Amatina. Blending lived experience with empowering advice, it offers strategies to help you understand your strengths, advocate for your needs and build a fulfilling work life. Whether you're newly diagnosed or years into your journey, this book reminds you: you belong.

www.ingramcontent.com/pod-product-compliance
Lightning Source LLC
LaVergne TN
LVHW090331210926
848480LV00004B/1370
9781919553863